I'll Build Us a Home

poems by

Emily Paige Wilson

Finishing Line Press
Georgetown, Kentucky

I'll Build Us a Home

Copyright © 2018 by Emily Paige Wilson
ISBN 978-1-63534-421-9 First Edition
All rights reserved under International and Pan-American Copyright Conventions. No part of this book may be reproduced in any manner whatsoever without written permission from the publisher, except in the case of brief quotations embodied in critical articles and reviews.

ACKNOWLEDGMENTS

Grateful acknowledgements are made to the editors of the following journals who published poems from this manuscript. Some previously published poems may appear here in a slightly different version.

Blue Monday Review: "I'll Burn the House We've Built"; "Love Spell for the Swamp"
Fourth & Sycamore: "We Fight About Having Children"
Heavy Feather Review: "Getting an IUD after Trump Becomes President-Elect"
Thrush: "I'll Build Us a Home (i)"; "I'll Build Us a Home (ii)"; "I'll Build Us a Home (iii)"
Tinderbox: "Friendship in Trump's America"
Underblong: "New Year's Eve on Market Street with My Best Friend's Son"
Voicemail Poems: "Love Spell for the Desert"

Publisher: Leah Maines
Editor: Christen Kincaid
Cover Art: Eli Sahm
Author Photo: Geniann Elliott
Cover Design: Elizabeth Maines McCleavy

Printed in the USA on acid-free paper.
Order online: www.finishinglinepress.com
         also available on amazon.com

Author inquiries and mail orders:
Finishing Line Press
P. O. Box 1626
Georgetown, Kentucky 40324
U. S. A.

Table of Contents

I'll Build Us a Home (i) 1

I'll Build Us a Home (ii) 2

Housewarming Incantation 3

Marriage Advice from My Mother 4

Our House Might Be Haunted 5

Love Spell for the Swamp 6

We Fight About Having Children 7

Getting an IUD after Trump Becomes the President-Elect 8

Friendship in Trump's America 9

Fear: Divorce 10

Questions to Ask Your Partner Besides "How Was Your Day?" .. 11

Roses de Nice on a Table 12

I'll Burn the House We've Built 13

Love Spell for the Beach 14

New Year's Eve on Market Street with My Best Friend's Son 16

Woman Holding a Balance 17

Solon, Iowa 19

How to Forgive 20

Love Spell for the Desert 21

I'll Build Us a Home (iii) 22

Late Shift 23

Because It Is Sometimes Hard to Say "I Love You," 24

We've Built Us a Home 25

—for Eli

"The lover's house improves with fire."—Rumi

I'll Build Us a Home (i)

of banded amethyst, basil, and bird
cages. You'll sleep beneath the sink,
where we'll keep soap and baby teeth.
We'll worship the purple morning
glories and pretend we planted them
outside the window on purpose. We'll
learn to read left handed. The trees
will apologize for never coming in,
blame it on their roots. We'll understand.
Our health will be consistent, no
sickness save the ache when August
scatters the cardinals. We'll spend
so much time together, we'll grow to only
speak of silver: the moon, the moths,
the bathwater we'll both forget to drain.

I'll Build Us a Home (ii)

of lilac, wings, and washing machines.
You'll wallpaper the bathroom
in prints of teacups and train whistles,
pinks that won't crease from shaving
cream and steam. Our pet jellyfish will
swim in jars of lactic acid, sweat we'll
collect from daily jogs. We'll never name
our floating family because sounds don't
adhere to wet bodies. You'll teach me
time is not sand but mud beneath
our feet, cool and thick. We'll smooth
salve over our scars and say, "Shhh,
This will keep the storms out." Though
you'll confuse the turnips and beets,
our pantry will always seem plenty.

Housewarming Incantation

One line for the excitement we try to scratch off
our skin like mosquito bites,
like the muggy August air we move our furniture in.
Our futures now a threadbare
couch and thrift store finds.

Two lines for how your father is delighted,
how mine has made no comment.

    One row of hematite arranged on the mantle. Smooth black stones
            with a hurricane sheen
        to ground our new house during storm season.

A fistful of sand for our Atlantic afternoons, trust exercises
done by the beach. My body
on your shoulders, you wade into the water as far as you can bear
my weight.
My skin closer to sky, closer to risk
of slipping without being able
to swim.

I'm sorry, father, but in this economy.

One cast iron cauldron for the meals we learn to cook one another,
the cilantro I introduce you to, the cartons of almond milk
and blueberries we buy in bulk.

A tough string of tongue clicks to starve off all the wasted
time we spent driving to and fro before, leaving
back porch lights on.

More sand for how the ocean laughs
at children like us, so concerned
with the safety

of just one body.

Marriage Advice from My Mother

Honey is a sugar substitute, not a name
to call your husband. Never ask explicitly
for sexual favors. Spell them out on the fridge
instead: a string of poetry magnets. *We are
a garden mess, pink music drunk on summer
mist, licked mean and sky-bent.* Paint
the walls of your children's rooms the color
of their greatest fear, soft grays and yellows.
Bring a bottle of Riesling to dinner
parties because it is what you like
to drink, never mind what the guests say
under their breath about sweetness. Watch
your weight; don't develop a sloppy silhouette.
Your husband will never get used to your
skin if it isn't spread thin and glossy
like a layer of apricot jam. Keep your concealer
underneath the sink. Prepare for the drowning
dreams, the reoccurring ones in which the water
rises to the roof. Carpets now carbon as an oil
slick, plaster walls drinking in the river's brown.
Your daughter will try to save the family
photos, but all you'll want is to jump
out the window, saying, *Not again, not again.*

Our House Might Be Haunted

Slight slant in the floorboards,
a tilt that teases doors from their hinges
with a slow creek, exposing our

bedroom to the hall's dark reach. Scent
that settles in the kitchen, mean rot of meat
we can't mask with lavender candles.

Lunatic curves of children's fingernails
we find unfurled in the carpet like shells
along the beach. The neighborhood

cat nursing a hole in its side, its red-edged skin
stretching with each step. The orb-weaver
spider we spun dizzy then dead with spray-

can poison, imagining it venomous, our thin
regrets woven into the now empty porch
corner. Hollow glass harp sounds

the Cape Fear River gasps out at night
as its bridge opens for boats to pass below.
And our neighbor who lives alone,

brings us groceries once a week. She
asks if the devil has spoken to us, too.
We shake our heads gently.

She turns back home, brow furrowed.
He walks, she says, *he walks.*
We stack her cans of creamed corn

near the trash, canister of ground
coffee unopened in our pantry.

Love Spell for the Swamp

If the swamp cannot be pleasant, let it be
humid—lush and low-hanging
with as much water as its lungs can hold.

If it can't be safe, let it serve
as a reminder: the quivering white
rabbit's tail, how nerves help us navigate
the world.

If it can't be
release, let it be the silent
sob of Spanish moss.

If it can't be beautiful,
let it be decadent—shellacked shades of emerald
brilliant on the bottle flies, ornate
curl of coppered leaves in early autumn

heat. If it can't be sweet, let it
be berries ruby and sour
in their dare

to be plucked. If it can't
be quiet, let it be the clink of shell
on turtle shell, tick on slick
human skin. The hum

of cicada and heron wings.
Let it be yellow light gentle
on the grass, like a lover's hand on a lover's chest
if it cannot be held itself.

We Fight About Having Children

Because my blood might calcify like stone,
clots of rose gypsum blocking circulation.
Because if my body must cause me pain,
cysts that burst on my Bartholin gland,
then I should at least be able to control
some of the delicious stretch and burn.
Because when I killed that spider, her
three egg sacks spun into a corner on our
porch, I knew some part of you would
never forgive me. Because I need to teach
a fresh mouth how to say moon and not fear
those strange sounds that sound so much
like want.

Getting an IUD after Trump Becomes the President-Elect

An empty vase has been placed near the sink.
An elongated bottle cut from bright cobalt glass,
slender neck stretched four or five inches high. It's my
distraction when the clamp's cold pinch starts to pull
and turn my stomach. I did not wish for this intimacy
with fear. My doctor's fingers caressing a cervix
that won't open, as if it knows how much power is placed
in keeping closed, in staying in control. As the spasms
crack my abdomen, smelling salts are placed on my chest.
I have never changed the contours of my body on behalf
of what someone else could take from it. To keep from
fainting, I exhale in counts of four. The world is over-
populated anyhow, I tell myself, and someone chose
not to fill the blue bottle with flowers, to let it just take
its own space.

Friendship in Trump's America

You're pregnant with your third daughter.
I see the baby bump on social media,
followed by posts about how protests are
unpatriotic, how women have lost no rights
yet. You're a good mother. I can tell
by the pictures of your two girls, golden-haired
and napping, smiles sappy with sleep.
Their bodies chose such an open posture
to plop down on those couch cushions,
and you are to thank for their sense of safety.
I type a timid response, ask if his comments
about snatching women without consent
encourage assault? You tell me that's ridiculous.
I'm entitled to an opinion, but that's absurd.
I wonder about the first girl he ever grabbed,
what color her eyes are. If her favorite animal
is a bird, or could ever be again.
Your two girls are sleeping on the couch,
and you're pregnant with your third.

Fear: Divorce

At night, my jaw recites its sleepless soundtrack of anxieties. I imagine its music like gravel, like gutter water realizing it will never be clean enough to drink. My dentist is the first to think of asking if it distracts you, the grind of molars with a mind of their own. Two teeth have chipped. I didn't expect my body to be so vocal about being broken, but I am warned: sensitivity, receding gums. I fear when the first tooth falls like a fleck of china from a floral cup, you'll be too polite to point it out. You'll sip slowly from the rim, no matter the crack that snags your lip. You'll want to leave but will be too afraid, the way you always wake right before you die in a dream. When you finally drive away, my mouth will be as empty as our house, all my vowels liquid now.

Questions to Ask Your Partner Besides "How Was Your Day?"

Do you also fear the silence that settles sometimes
    between us at breakfast, tolerant as a fog? Words

heavy as headlights in their reaching? Do you green with a forestry
    of regrets as your body grows forgetful of fingers

other than ours? Can I show you what we take
    for granted: the strangeness of a sunset; orange

veins tangled in trees, a dime-sized disc and its synonyms
    for silver? Would you rather never again touch the jealous

sculpture of a lover's jaw or be milled through
    the machinery of praise after a hard day? Tell me

how long since you've read back our love
    letters, a literacy both foolish and proud

in its impossible theater? When was the last laugh
    that caught you off path, blew past you

panicked and damaged as a harvest-colored wind chime
    and wasn't it mine?

Roses de Nice on a Table

What woman so disturbed
me, as she walked down
the street, trailing the scent
of lilac like a lace veil

that I now collect small glass
bottles of perfume, the blooms
of jasmine and lavender, to wear
my wilting on my wrist?

When I told him I'd leave, I didn't
tell him at all. Roses grow
in two groups: climbers and shrubs.

Ballerina roses can be both.

I'll Burn the House We've Built

You'll return to find the strange orange
comfort of heat. I'll say the candles started
to speak to me in their language of wax and wick.
Shoeless in singed grass, I'll clasp your golden
frog paperweight—the only thing I'll spare
since frogs cannot sense gradual threats:
a pot of water boiling, dishes unclean in the sink,
these feelings similar to the flu. But it won't be
anyone's fault, though the starlings will blame
themselves as they observe from the branches.
Our birds took their chances trusting
the sun; now they won't know how to tell
day from night because of this light, won't
sleep for weeks. I'll watch the blaze lay
waste to the beams of our house as casually
as a sunbather pulls off thin layers of burned
skin. You'll see the pink in my sweating cheeks,
wonder when you lost focus of my face.
As the sparks finally lay fallow, I'll offer you
my hand. Palm in palm, we'll rummage in the ruins
beneath a moon other than honey: wolf moon,
winter, hunter.

Love Spell for the Beach

If the beach feels home
to no one—tourists who prefer to take
pictures and leave; shores that erode slow
                                   as bad habits;
                small seagrass gardens passing
by without roots—
    then let the beach watch at night
for the moon: its white globe
glossed on water like a door knob,
our first encounter with any house.

        If the waves feel unheard,
let them   reconsider speech.
It's not the roar   of reaching
       and retrieving that convinces us to listen.
                It's the ocean's own wrecked
handwriting, seaweed and sewage
washed on shore, an incomplete
        Morse code of debris and foam.

If the ocean ever feels bloated
with salt, let it take solace
      that it's not fresh
water: too fearful to cause a burn
in the back of a throat,   to ask
                another body
                      to hold all of it. If

    the landscape stretches itself plain,
        an unending strip of beige,
let it remember it is why,   of all colors,
                  language gives last
a name to blue—cornflower and cobalt
   hues, turquoise caught
   in between green and sky—because which
sounds could be used to summon the sea?

If the water must be exposed,
its surface warm and floated on,
at least its depths
        let us believe
        in creatures who carry on their lives
without the need to be seen.

                            And if the shore sees itself
      as uncomfortable—only shards of shells
    and microscopic rock, bits of worn
down beach glass—let it sense how like skin

sand is, blustered and broken, human.

New Year's Eve on Market Street with My Best Friend's Son

Ezra has only begun to mouth sounds
that meet the ear as words in the past
two months. We take him down
to the river to watch the fireworks
explode into their own red and green
vowels. He's just learned boat and moans
the *o* as if his tiny body knows what it is
to sink. Situated on my hip as the night
cries phosphorus and copper, Ezra is caught
among the colors, his pupils a wide glass
cut to hold the moment. As he waves
his hands in tiny excitement, a glove
falls to the ground. Astounded by the sharp
sting of cold air, he stares now at his fingers.
Ow, ow until the hand is once again
covered. I wonder who has taught him
to first feel unknown sensations as pain,
the probability that it was me.

Woman Holding a Balance

How does she so softly relax her face, draped
in a white cotton bonnet, shadows suggesting

a hand holding her cheek? What does she think
as she steadies the balance, ready to weigh

the worth of the jewelry below? I want her
to know this is how anxiety makes me

feel daily: strained from the weight of holding
two opposing emotions, always and equally.

Sometimes the fight is with my own skin.
Luminous in some light, then uneven

as craquelure in others, aged and enough
to convince me I'll lose love when I lose

youth. Sometimes the burden that threatens
to overturn the balance is a type of love itself.

One side sways with thoughts that I deserve better
than my lover; the other, that he deserves better

than me. A woman who won't let discontent
settle in, won't force a silver chain to fit

over her head and then blame the clasp for breaking.
All my mind's fights, though, are really the same

pained conversations between fear and faith.
I want the peace this woman possesses, two

invisible birds of equal weight perched patiently
on each pan of her balance. Perhaps that is why

she bends her ear slightly to one side, to hear
the music of her own making. My mind is never

that quiet. The woman will eventually weigh the gold,
calculate the cost of the blue fabric billowing

on the table before her. I think of the pearls
she'll touch, their lazy luster on the throat.

The same cold, heavy weight apprehension
presses into the chest. A distraction for her

fingers to fidget with instead of bringing
the balance to a fixed position. It has taken me

so long to realize what the nerves never want you to
see: both of the balance's pans are always empty.

Solon, Iowa

Patchwork is an imprecise
metaphor for these fields. We
have been driving among them
all afternoon and I've seen nothing
to suggest of the careful stitching
of a quilt, the intent to keep
a body warm. The earth is not
worn cloth, an invitation to lie down.
The ground does not care if we are
comfortable. This morning I
cried for two hours in a hotel shower
for no reason besides a feeling
as big and empty as a field.
Eli wants to know what's wrong,
but sad is such a small word
outside the mouth. He tells me it
will pass, that vague pain always
passes by like hurried landscapes seen
blurred from the passenger side. So I
look out the window for something to hold
onto. Maybe how the fields unfold
golden, if not soft. Or how the heavy sun
sinks orange into the wicker basket
the black branches weave around it,
the sky's last blue dare dimming now.
How the small road sign reading
Lingle Creek sounds so much like *linger*.

How to Forgive

Anger is the wet, white-tiled bathroom floor, linoleum's cold
knock on your chapped heels as you step from the shower.
What a strange shade of red, the beard he braids until it breaks,

tangled into accidental wicker baskets that block the drain.
What a strange custom, two bodies using the same space to clean
themselves, its small comfort and suffocation. Your own hair

trapped on the tile appears as thin and difficult
as a cursive lowercase z. Why is it always
twilight—the towel's cotton touch, mirror

steamed of its meaning—when these white tiles
ask you to graph your happiness from numb
to not, the need to ask at all. Think of all

the copper coins shipwrecked on his skin,
how long it would take to name them
with a number. The counting might outlast

the anger, how the answer would still be
smaller than all the couples who have come
before you, showering in their same small

spaces, nursing hurts they can't name either.
All those miraculous, failing pairs
dripping on the bathroom floor.

Love Spell for the Desert

If the desert cannot be settled,
let it be anxious and alert—its worry
a sandstorm.
              Let it cover in protective
              dust what it loves. If

the desert can't be hospitable, let it
take solace in what it can offer: no
one appreciates water without
first experiencing thirst. All myths
     begin with dirt—let the desert remember
this if it must be homesick.

If the desert finds itself
              too vast to keep
          track of, let it know it is a canvas—
   night paints expansive its stars and black
glass, the scent of cactus flower.

          If its scorched earth can't be
fertile, let it feel it is not
alone—the desert lark in its cracked
jacket of mud, the sand-speckled
flesh of the spade-foot toad—let it know

camouflage is finding safety in family resemblance.
If the desert is ever accused of storing secrets,
              let it always refer back to its blue
scar of sky. How could a place

       afraid to share itself hold this much
       open? If the desert can't be lush,
let it burn metallic like molten
copper ore. Some people wait for

       the rust and flame of sunset every day,
but the desert was born with this orange
      in its skin.

I'll Build Us a Home (iii)

of pollen, plaster, and copper wind
chimes. Your brothers will bring us
linen pajamas with each visit. We won't
know how to say, *Please, the closets
are full.* You'll carve spoons from
selenite; we'll re-center our souls
with each bowl of cereal. You'll teach
me about constellations by spilling
curry on our dark kitchen counters,
swirling shapes in the spices. I'll still
scratch your ears, even after you drop
my favorite perfume—the scent of fresh
peonies and pepper—glass scattered
—but I'll ask you to keep your hands
unwashed for as long as you can bear.

Late Shift

Every night when I come home
from work, we slow

dance in the kitchen. Maybe
because

after all those people, I just want
one person.

Maybe because we've been told
to dance

romantic near an unclean
sink

by the poets. Or maybe
because

it's the warmest room
in the house

when we open the oven
to avoid

turning up the heat.

Because It Is Sometimes Hard to Say "I Love You,"

I want to tell you this instead: watching "Days
of Heaven" that night, I loved how you loved
those shots of wheat fields: wide as wingspans,
hollow as the bones that hold them up. Camera
panning the landscape so expansive, you could
imagine no other job worth doing than this:
cinematography the only way to kiss
another's body. Shadows scattered on our walls,
pulsing and private as the cursive of children.
Sometimes I think we are the only ones
who've ever felt this way, though the movie
makes this an impossible thought—
the leading man loves his leading lady enough
to pretend he doesn't, day in and day out.
We all know such complications and risks.
We were burrowed in the couch that night,
scent of fir flickering from the candle tin.
Cocooned inside our body heat, I knew
I could be a red dwarf on the verge of imploding
and feel no fear if it meant radiating such warmth.
I'm not sure that's how stars work, but I'm trying
to embrace the unknown, not to hold onto what I can't
predict, except the thickness of your arms
around mine, how my skin translates all
the languages that lay sleeping on our tongues
for your skin, and your skin does the same.
He dies in the film, and she steals
away back into the grain and its gold.
Sometimes I still think we are
the only ones, foolishly.

We've Built Us a Home

of yarn, soap, and yard sale spoons.
Afternoons, I nap on the warm brick
of your back. Evenings, you baste everything
we bake in brown sugar, though we don't
cook as often as we told the tomato plants
we would. You've grown a beard since
August. When we decorated the mantle
with dried elderberry branches, your jawline
wanted adornment, too. The landlady
won't let us paint the walls, so I bathe them
in moss and mauve in my mind. We pack
mugs full of tea for each friend that leaves
the city, burn essential oils before the storms.
Rosemary so the river won't rise, blood
orange for the rent. I water the secluded
succulents in their clay pots, how the dirt
cracks and calls like a bell in thirst. We love
this sound because it keeps us happy,
because the smallest things can still surprise us.

Emily Paige Wilson's poetry has been nominated for Best of the Net, *Best New Poets*, and two Pushcart Prizes. Her work can be found in *The Adroit Journal, Hayden's Ferry Review, PANK,* and *Thrush,* among others, and has won or placed in contests hosted by *The Indiana Review, Mid-American Review, Tinderbox,* North Carolina State University, and Oberlin College. She earned her MFA from the University of North Carolina Wilmington, where she received the Kert Green and Brauer fellowships. She currently lives in Wilmington and works as an English adjunct and writing tutor at local community colleges.

www.ingramcontent.com/pod-product-compliance
Lightning Source LLC
LaVergne TN
LVHW041512070426
835507LV00012B/1508